UIC

Dorothea Lange

Robyn Montana Turner

Little, Brown and Company
Boston New York Toronto London

For my sister, Carrie Beth, a photojournalist

ACKNOWLEDGMENTS

I'd like to extend my grateful appreciation to the many individuals who influenced the development of this series and this book, including my editors, Maria Modugno and Hilary M. Breed, for tenaciously seeing this book through to completion; Virginia A. Creeden for gathering permissions for the images; Therese Heyman and the staff of the Dorothea Lange Collection at the Oakland Museum for helping me research Lange's photographs and documents; my parents for keeping cameras and darkroom equipment in my childhood home; my daughter, Tara, for reviewing the manuscript; and Timothy Koock for offering moral support.

First Edition

Quotation on page 3 and back of jacket from "Dorothea Lange," by Daniel Dixon, in *Modern Photography*, December 1952.

Library of Congress Cataloging-in-Publication Data

Turner, Robyn.
   Dorothea Lange / Robyn Montana Turner. — 1st ed.
     p. cm. — (Portraits of women artists for children)
   ISBN 0-316-85656-8
   1. Lange, Dorothea — Juvenile literature. 2. Women photographers — United States Biography — Juvenile literature. [1. Lange, Dorothea. 2. Photographers. 3. Women — Biography.] I. Title. II. Series: Portraits of women artists.
   TR140.L3T87 1994
   7701'.92 — dc20
   [B]   93-42573

10 9 8 7 6 5 4 3 2 1

SC

Published simultaneously in Canada by Little, Brown & Company (Canada) Limited

Printed in Hong Kong

There I was, sitting on a big rock — and right in the middle of it, with the thunder bursting and the wind whistling, it came to me that what I had to do was to take pictures and concentrate upon people, only people, all kinds of people, people who paid me and people who didn't.

— Dorothea Lange

4

Dorothea Lange

(dor-uh-THEE-uh LANG)
(1895–1965)

Just 150 years ago, only a few women in the world had become well known as artists. Since then many women have been recognized for their artwork. Today some very famous artists are women.

Nowadays both boys and girls are encouraged to become great artists. They may attend the best art schools and study with the finest art teachers.

But let's imagine that you could go back in time to the turn of the twentieth century — about a hundred years ago. As a young person growing up in America at that time, you might wonder why women artists in your country have only just recently been allowed to attend the best schools of art. You might question why women artists are not welcome at social gatherings where male artists learn from each other by discussing new ideas about art. You might be surprised to discover that women have just recently been permitted to look at nude models to help them learn how to portray the human figure. And you might be disappointed to learn that most young girls are not encouraged to become great painters, sculptors, or photographers.

Soon after that time, several American women took a chance in the arts and, despite the odds against their success, became well-known photographers. In 1919, when women gained the right to vote, one of those young women established her own photography studio in San Francisco. Her name was Dorothea Lange, and she, too, would become well known as an artist. Today her photographs are seen throughout the world.

Rondal Partridge. **Dorothea Lange.** *1934. Copyright © Rondal Partridge, 1993.* This photograph was taken by one of the sons of Dorothea Lange's close friend Roi Partridge.

1041 Bloomfield Street, Hoboken, New Jersey.
Courtesy of the Dorothea Lange Collection, The Oakland Museum. Gift of Paul S. Taylor.

On May 25, 1895, a baby girl named Dorothea Margaretta Nutzhorn was born to Henry Martin Nutzhorn and Joan Lange Nutzhorn in a brownstone row house in Hoboken, New Jersey. Dorothea was named after her father's mother. The name means "gift of God" in Greek.

Many immigrants lived in Hoboken, including Dorothea's grandparents, who had emigrated from Germany. Her parents had both been born in the United States. Her father was a lawyer, and her mother sang in recitals. Several of Dorothea's uncles were lithographers, or printmakers, who had trained in Germany and set up a business in America. Little did they know that their young niece would later become a visual artist, too, and set up her own photography business.

When Dorothea was six years old, her brother, Martin, was born. Life seemed good for the freckled, fine-boned young girl with greenish-blue eyes. She enjoyed playing with her new baby brother. A year later, when she was seven, however, her life took an unexpected and unfortunate turn. Dorothea was stricken with polio. As a result, muscles in her right leg stopped growing, and it soon became a bit shorter than the left one, causing her to limp. She needed shoes a half size smaller for her right foot. It upset Dorothea when children called her "Limpy." Even more, her mother hurt her feelings by acting ashamed of Dorothea's handicap. When friends were near, Joan would whisper to her daughter, "Now, walk as well as you can!" For the rest of her life, Dorothea would walk with a limp. She would accept her condition, although it would always haunt her.

Dorothea's mother was an attractive woman. She usually wore her reddish-brown hair tied back in a knot. Her skin was rosy and freckled, and her facial features were pronounced. Her senses were alive, as she loved to experience all kinds of tastes, smells, and sights. She collected records and books. She was concerned about people who were treated unfairly, and she tried to help them. Dorothea loved her mother, but she did not like Joan's reluctance to make decisions. She felt her mother cared too much about what others thought and tried to please too many people.

As a child, Dorothea felt love and affection for her father. She often read from a book of Shakespeare's plays. Her father and mother would tease her affectionately about such grown-up reading, then quiz her about the plays. When Dorothea was ten, as a special treat, her father took her to a performance of *A Midsummer Night's Dream*. He held her on his shoulders so she could see over the crowd.

When Dorothea was twelve, Henry abandoned the family forever, leaving Joan the sole support. Dorothea never talked about why her parents separated or why her father left. For the rest of her life, she would rarely speak of her father and would always carry deep pain concerning his absence. Eventually Dorothea would drop her father's name and take on her mother's maiden name. Instead of Dorothea Nutzhorn, she became Dorothea Lange.

In 1907, Joan found a job as a librarian at a branch of the New York City Public Library on the Lower East Side of Manhattan Island. Although she was bringing home money, she still needed some help. So to ease the financial burden, she took Dorothea and Martin with her to live with her mother, Sophie Vottler Lange, in Hoboken.

Grandma Sophie was moody and difficult, and she drank too much. Yet she was talented. She was a superb dressmaker, always looking for perfection. Both she and Dorothea had an artistic eye, which

Dorothea and Her Brother, Martin. *Collection of Helen Dixon.*

helped them see beauty in ordinary things. For example, she told young Dorothea that of all the things that were beautiful in the world, there was nothing finer than an orange. Dorothea knew exactly what she meant.

Dorothea's artistic eye was apparent to others as well. One day, she stared out the window at the blue sky, wooden fences, red brick buildings, and rows of clean laundry hanging out to dry. She even noticed the rusty squeaking sounds the clotheslines made. She commented about this ordinary neighborhood scene, "To me, that's beautiful." Her friend standing behind her responded, "To you, everything is beautiful." This remark startled Dorothea, because she had always thought that everyone saw things as she did. Now she realized that perhaps she had a special talent.

During the first two years of living with Grandma Sophie, Dorothea and Joan rode the ferry from Hoboken to Manhattan early in the morning five days a week. Then, from the landing at Christopher Street, they walked across town to a Lower East Side neighborhood packed with thousands of struggling immigrants who poured off Ellis Island. Railway cars roared over their heads as they listened to the many languages spoken by the people on the streets — mainly Yiddish, spoken by the Jewish immigrants from central and eastern Europe, but also Chinese, Italian, Bohemian, Hungarian, and English with an Irish accent. Smells of pickles, garlic, and herring from sidewalk pushcarts competed with the stench of sewage beneath the streets. A penny would buy a ride on a horse-drawn merry-go-round or a newspaper at the corner newsstand.

In this crowded district of New York City stood the branch library. Joan's twelve-dollars-per-week salary there was double the average family pay in that community. Instead of attending classes, half of the school-age children worked in factories or on the streets to help their families survive.

At the nearby Public School 62, where 95 percent of the students were from homes where English was not the main language spoken, Dorothea felt like an outsider. Seventh and eighth grades were not easy for her. Although she was bright and quick to catch on, she could hardly keep up with her busy classmates. They were high achievers, eager to better their skills so they could work their way out of the poverty-stricken environment. Girls and boys attended separate classes. The school was known for its advanced ideas in education and its experienced teachers.

After school, Dorothea usually walked to the library where her mother worked. Waiting for Joan to get off work, Dorothea explored her interest in art as she pored through art books in the library. Twice each week, however, Joan worked the night shift, so Dorothea went home alone after school. She walked through the roughest part of New York City, the Bowery, for nearly a mile. Stepping over drunken men on filthy sidewalks, the twelve-year-old girl was scared. But she taught herself how to make her way through the dangerous streets without drawing attention to herself. Later, as a photographer of people in difficult situations, she would use this skill again, ignoring others' glances and avoiding eye contact in order to fade into any crowd.

When Dorothea finished at P.S. 62, she attended Wadleigh High School, uptown in Harlem. Her best subjects were English, drawing, and music, although the school gave no special attention to the arts.

During these years, Dorothea became bored with school and often did not attend classes. Instead, she and her friend Florence "Fronsie" Ahlstrom strolled

Metropolitan Museum of Art. *1917. Courtesy of The Metropolitan Museum of Art.* Dorothea and Fronsie liked to visit the Metropolitan Museum of Art to see which artists were being exhibited there.

through Central Park, listened to free concerts, and saw exhibits at the Museum of Natural History, the Metropolitan Museum of Art, and the Art Students League. Dorothea became an observer of the city, noticing the many sights and sounds and, most of all, the variety of people.

At home, Grandma Sophie's drinking habit had grown worse. She often yelled at Dorothea, hit her, and ordered her around. Joan was too timid to do anything about it. So Dorothea stayed away from home a lot. She would wander the streets of the city alone or with Fronsie. Toward the end of her life, Lange would fondly recall those days of exploration. She would say she was self-taught about life — through constantly watching and trying to discover why things happen the way they do.

Despite the many classes she missed, Dorothea managed to graduate from Wadleigh High School in June 1913. What would she do next? Her mother believed Dorothea should pursue a career that would offer financial security, such as teaching. But Dorothea's fascination with observing the sights of the city led her to think about exploring a career in photography instead. Dorothea announced her plans of becoming a photographer, even though she had no camera and had never made a photograph. She simply knew that was what she wanted to do. To please her mother, however, she now enrolled in the New York Training School for Teachers.

One summer day, she noticed a striking collection of portrait photographs in a display window on Fifth Avenue. She went inside and persuaded Arnold Genthe to hire her as his apprentice. She soon discovered that he was a famous photographer. Genthe had moved from San Francisco, where he had photographed celebrities — presidents, actors, writers, musicians. He had also taken informal pictures of people on the streets of Chinatown and of San Francisco's 1906 earthquake and fire.

Lange worked in Genthe's studio each day after school for fifteen dollars a week. With Genthe's other assistants, she printed proofs of the film that Genthe had used to photograph his subjects. If the proofs showed white spots from specks of dust, she corrected the negatives by carefully spotting them with india ink. She learned to mount and frame the finished portraits.

To show his appreciation for Lange's good work, Genthe gave her a camera. By now, she knew photography was her passion. To her mother's disappointment, she quit her teacher training to pursue a full-time career as a photographer.

Now Lange was free to spend all of her time studying photography. She worked in several studios training as an apprentice, and she learned to operate the large 8 x 10 cameras. One day in 1916 at her twelve-dollar-per-week job, she received an unexpected assignment. Mrs. Beatty, the studio owner, had just lost her professional portrait photographer, so she took a chance and sent Lange to photograph the wealthy Brokaw family. Lange's steady nerves saw her through, and everyone agreed that the resulting portraits were outstanding. This lucky break launched Lange's career as a portrait photographer.

During the next two years, she took a course in photography at Columbia University and set up a darkroom in the chicken coop behind the family home. She earned enough money in her growing career as a photographer to help with family expenses.

In January 1918, when Lange was twenty-two, she and Fronsie Ahlstrom decided to test their independence. With just $140, they set out to go

Art Students League of New York. *1983.*
The Art Students League, which continues today, offers classes in the visual arts to the general public. Many of America's best artists have studied there.

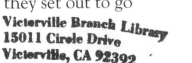

Dorothea Lange. **Maynard
Dixon.** *1920s. Courtesy of the
Dorothea Lange Collection,
The Oakland Museum. Gift of
Paul S. Taylor.*
One day as she worked in
her basement darkroom,
Lange heard clicking
footsteps in her studio above.
She later married Maynard
Dixon, the man whose
cowboy boots had turned her
ear.

around the world. First they traveled from New York to New Orleans by boat. Then they took a train west that stopped in Texas and New Mexico. On May 18, 1918, they arrived in San Francisco.

On that same day, their money was stolen. When the world travelers discovered they had only four dollars and some change remaining, they set about to find work in San Francisco.

By the next day, Fronsie had a job with Western Union, and Dorothea was hired at the photo-finishing department of a dry-goods store named Marsh and Company. Working behind the counter taking orders, she met many San Franciscans who were involved in photography. Marsh's counter was the beginning of a new life for Dorothea.

A couple who would become her lifelong friends were the photographer Imogen Cunningham and printmaker Roi Partridge. Through them, she was introduced to San Francisco's painters, writers, photographers, and other artists. Soon she joined a camera club to have access to a darkroom. A friend in the club offered to finance a portrait studio for her, so she set up shop at 540 Sutter Street. She built a darkroom in the basement. The studio became a gathering place for her friends, who relaxed with tea and conversation around the fireplace. Before long, she became the most popular portrait photographer among the cultural leaders of San Francisco.

One day in Lange's studio, Roi Partridge introduced her to a painter of the Western wilderness, Maynard Dixon. Lange found him handsome in his cowboy boots and Western clothes. Lange, too, cast a striking impression. She dressed in comfortable clothes that reflected her artful ways. She sported heavy silver jewelry — a squash-blossom necklace and a Navajo ring and bracelet.

Lange and Dixon fell in love and decided to be

married. On March 21, 1920, their wedding took place in Lange's studio with Fronsie Ahlstrom as the maid of honor and Roi Partridge as best man.

During the next few years, Lange often traveled in the West with her husband on his sketching trips. She took many pictures of him, such as the medium close-up shot *Maynard Dixon*.

In the summer of 1923, they joined a collector of Dixon's paintings, Anita Baldwin McClaughry, on an excursion to the Navajo and Hopi country in the Southwest. Dixon painted while Lange photographed. *Hopi Indian* is an extreme close-up portrait. The camera lens captured the shiny and porous texture of the subject's skin, along with the deep lines that reveal his personal history. Through this private point of view, Lange invited the viewer to feel a special closeness to the Hopi.

Dorothea Lange. **Hopi Indian.** *New Mexico, c. 1923. Courtesy of the Dorothea Lange Collection, The Oakland Museum. Gift of Paul S. Taylor.*
On her trip through the Southwest, Lange photographed many Native Americans. Lange chose to portray this man with an intimate close-up shot.

Dorothea Lange. **Mexican American.** *San Francisco, 1928. Courtesy of the Dorothea Lange Collection, The Oakland Museum. Gift of Paul S. Taylor.*
Lange's talent as a portrait photographer grew with her experience both in the studio and during her travels with Maynard Dixon. *Mexican American* captures the life within a small child's eyes.

Although the artistic couple enjoyed being together, complications soon arose. Dixon brought to the marriage his ten-year-old daughter, who did not get along with Lange. In 1927, after seven years of disharmony, seventeen-year-old Constance finally moved away from home.

Lange and Dixon had their own children as well. In 1925, Daniel Rhodes Dixon was born, followed by a second son, John Eaglefeather Dixon, in 1928.

While the boys were small, Lange managed to find time for both mothering and photographing. She sometimes combined the two by taking pictures of her boys, such as *Mother's Day Daisies*. This image of John's small fist holding a bouquet represents every child who suddenly remembers that today is Mother's Day.

Dixon continued full-time with his artwork, however, and was gone from home a lot. In order to keep her business afloat, Lange placed the young boys with other families for months at a time. The decision was a difficult one, but she was as devoted to her photography as Dixon was to his painting. In fact, Lange kept a remarkably successful business going. *Mexican American* is another example of a photograph Lange shot during those years.

Late in the summer of 1929, the family took a vacation to the countryside in California. Dixon enjoyed watching Lange photograph their sons in natural surroundings. She was moving away from her studio walls into a new frontier. In an approach called documentary photography, she would combine the artful quality of photography with its function of recording historical events.

It was during this trip that she unexpectedly experienced a spiritual awakening. One afternoon during a quiet moment alone, she thought about why her landscape shots were not as pleasing as were her photographs of her family. Suddenly she noticed a thunderstorm piling up. Many years later, she explained to her son Daniel, "When it broke, there I was, sitting on a big rock — and right in the middle of it, with the thunder bursting and the wind whistling, it came to me that what I had to do was to take pictures and concentrate upon people, only people, all kinds of people, people who paid me and people who didn't."

Dorothea Lange. **Mother's Day Daisies.** *San Francisco, 1934. Courtesy of the Dorothea Lange Collection, The Oakland Museum. Gift of Paul S. Taylor.*
This photograph is of Lange's young son John.

Dorothea Lange. **Katten Portrait.** *San Francisco, 1934. Courtesy of the Dorothea Lange Collection, The Oakland Museum. Gift of Paul S. Taylor.*
Among Lange's customers in San Francisco, the Kattens enjoyed extended-family portraits, in which grandchildren posed with grandparents.

The family returned to San Francisco in the early fall of 1929. On October 24, the stock market in New York City crashed, marking the beginning of the Great Depression. When the stocks lost their value, the entire nation changed. By the winter of 1929, banks had lost money and production of goods had slowed down. This disaster caused millions of workers to lose their jobs. Many people couldn't afford enough food to feed their families. They shuffled into breadlines to receive a simple meal free of charge.

Many wealthy art collectors stopped buying paintings and commissioning portraits such as the *Katten Portrait.* Among other artists, Lange and Dixon were hit hard. They gathered up their boys and drove to Taos, New Mexico, where there was a small community of artists. They stayed for seven months. Dixon continued to ignore his parental duties and painted full-time. Lange took care of the family and sometimes found the time to photograph people of Taos. The primitive village tucked away in the mountains seemed somewhat removed from the burdens of the Great Depression.

When the foursome arrived back in San Francisco, they saw that the city was suffering. Although their family had enough to eat, they had to give up their house. Lange moved into the studio she had taken on Montgomery Street, and Dixon moved into his studio three doors down. John, four, and Dan, seven, were placed in a nearby boarding school so that Lange and Dixon could continue their careers. Lange would always carry with her the pain she felt when she and Dixon said good-bye to the boys after weekend visits.

In her studio, Lange continued to make prints, signing and dating them, for the few people who could still afford such luxuries. But one day, as she stared out her second-floor window at the masses of jobless Americans who wandered aimlessly, she knew she must follow her spiritual path. She took her camera down the stairs and onto the streets to photograph even those people who couldn't pay her.

Lange didn't know what to expect from the anxious crowd. She called upon her own girlhood memories of the Bowery and again assumed an invisible face for protection. She walked to a breadline organized by a wealthy woman called the White Angel. Suddenly Lange discovered that photographing people outside her studio was unlike her usual task. No longer could she pose subjects. Now she must select them unposed from their general surroundings. She was quickly becoming a social observer.

Barbara Puorro Galasso.
4 x 5 Speed Graflex Camera. *George Eastman House.*
Lange usually worked with a large camera called a 4 x 5 Graflex, similar to the one shown above. It was much heavier than modern-day cameras.

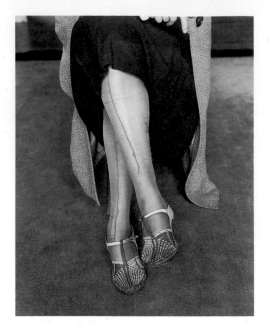

Dorothea Lange. **Mended Stockings.** *San Francisco, 1934. Courtesy of the Dorothea Lange Collection, The Oakland Museum. Gift of Paul S. Taylor.*
Mended stockings were common during the Great Depression. In what way are they a sign of the time?

Within minutes, Lange photographed *White Angel Breadline*, which would become one of the lasting images of the Depression era. The strong social message centers around the unshaven old man, who leans on a rail, with a tin can between his arms. His clenched hands and downturned mouth show the bitterness he feels. His hunched back is turned to others who, like himself, await a free meal. The composition of the image shows the artist's technical skill. Her subject stands near the center, with his hat and hands highlighted to emphasize his presence. Diagonal lines and triangular shapes strengthen the composition.

Lange's new way of photographing people, unposed and in their natural surroundings, caught the attention of the well-known photographer Willard Van Dyke. He exhibited the photographs in his studio in Oakland, California, near San Francisco. Through this exhibit, Lange met someone who would become an important part of her life. Paul Taylor, a university economics professor, was impressed by the exhibit and contacted her. He thought her style of photographing people in their environments would complement his own writing projects.

Together Lange and Taylor surveyed the struggles of the migrant workers in the state of California. Farmers there had always hired low-wage temporary workers, usually unmarried men, who moved regularly within the state to help harvest fruit and vegetable crops. But by 1934, a sudden gush of thousands of homeless families was pouring into California in hopes of finding migrant work. During the next two years Taylor wrote about the living conditions of those families who had left their drought-stricken homes in other states, while Lange photographed them.

Dorothea Lange. **White Angel Breadline.** *San Francisco, 1933. Courtesy of the Dorothea Lange Collection, The Oakland Museum. Gift of Paul S. Taylor.*

The appeal of this classic photograph of the Great Depression rests both in the way it is composed and in the message it conveys.

Dorothea Lange and Paul Taylor. *St. George, Utah, 1935. Courtesy of the Dorothea Lange Collection, The Oakland Museum. Gift of Paul S. Taylor.*
Lange and Taylor traveled together to migrant camps, where people needed food, clothing, and better shelter. Their reports about the camps brought the problems to the attention of government agencies and the public.

Their reports influenced the state to build camps where the migrant families could live while they harvested crops. The reports also helped start a similar project of the federal government in Washington, D.C., later to be called the Farm Security Administration (FSA). For several years, Lange and Taylor worked together as government employees on these state and federal projects. Taylor interviewed the migrants, and Lange photographed them. The FSA hired other writers and photographers as well, to document living conditions across the United States. In this way, Lange and others created a visual record of the Great Depression. In exchange, they earned salaries and improved their photography skills as they experimented with different subjects, lighting conditions, background considerations, and other challenges. This approach, of photographing people in their immediate surroundings, is known as documentary photography.

Dorothea Lange. **Child in Pea Pickers Camp.** *Near Stockton, California, 1935. Courtesy of the Dorothea Lange Collection, The Oakland Museum. Gift of Paul S. Taylor.*
Although many children in the migrant camps were unhappy from poor living conditions, this girl seems to have found something to smile about.

Meanwhile, Lange and Dixon had grown apart. Their marriage had undergone too much strain from the pressure of trying to combine a family life with their individual careers. In October 1935, they divorced. She married her coworker Paul Taylor in December. This marriage would be strong. For the next thirty years, Lange and Taylor would work together on projects to document events of their time. Among the photographs she took in the mid-1930s is *Child in Pea Pickers Camp*, which shows the living conditions of migrant workers.

One cold, wet evening in March 1936, Lange was driving back to San Francisco from a full day of photographing migrant workers in the fields. She passed a handmade road sign that read "Pea Pickers Camp."

Something made her stop and turn the car around. She was following her innermost feelings — her instinct — rather than her reason. On the soggy grounds of the migrant camp, she parked the car, got out, and walked straight over to a hungry and desperate-looking mother. Lange felt as though they were drawn to each other like magnets.

Dorothea Lange. **Migrant Mother.** *Nipomo, California, 1936. Courtesy of the Dorothea Lange Collection, The Oakland Museum. Gift of Paul S. Taylor.*
When Lange drove into the pea pickers' camp, she spotted the migrant mother's lean-to tent.

21

Día de las Madres. *1964.*
Courtesy of the Dorothea
Lange Collection, The Oakland
Museum and Bohemia
Venezuela, Caracas.
This drawing of *Migrant*
Mother appeared in a Cuban
magazine published in
Venezuela.

Malik. **Poverty Is a Crime.**
1972. Pencil drawing.
Courtesy of the Dorothea
Lange Collection, The Oakland
Museum. Gift of Paul S.
Taylor.
Migrant Mother has become
so well known that its image
has been adapted to other
cultures and causes as well.

Without much discussion, the woman agreed to
let Lange photograph her with her hungry children
in their lean-to tent. Lange believed that she
somehow knew that the pictures might help the
woman. The pea crop there had frozen, everyone was
out of work, and the only food was the frozen
vegetables and birds that the children had killed.

Lange worked fast, her usual approach. And, as
always, she gained great satisfaction in shooting the
pictures. When she returned home that night, she
developed the film and took the prints to the editor
of the *San Francisco News*. She told him that the pea
pickers in Nipomo were starving. The editor quickly
sent the story out to newspapers across the country.
Several days later, the *News* reported that the federal
government was rushing twenty thousand pounds of
food to feed the starving migrants.

Both Lange and the migrant mother had
successfully followed their instincts. The mother
received food for her family. And Lange received
praise for her outstanding photograph, which she
entitled *Migrant Mother*. Other publications quickly
printed the image. Five years later, it was exhibited
in New York City's Museum of Modern Art, and
today it is known throughout the world.

By now Lange and Taylor were used to asking
friends to keep Daniel and John, along with Taylor's
three children from a former marriage, while they
worked. On weekends, they would gather up the
children. These reunions were painful, yet joyous,
occasions, since everyone missed being together.

In May 1936, Lange traveled with Taylor to the
East to meet with her supervisor, Roy Stryker, in
Washington, D.C. Stryker usually offered detailed
instructions about her assignments. Nevertheless, he
trusted Lange's artistic sense, even though he
sometimes bristled at her independent solutions. She

would set out on field trips in the general direction he had suggested, but with no plan of what to shoot. As photographer Willard Van Dyke said of her approach to assignments, Lange tried to keep her mind open like a roll of sensitive, unexposed film. Soon she would see something worth looking into,

Dorothea Lange. **Migrant Mother.** *Nipomo, California, 1936. Courtesy of the Dorothea Lange Collection, The Oakland Museum. Gift of Paul S. Taylor.* This image has become Lange's trademark.

Dorothea Lange. **Hoe Culture.** *Near Anniston, Alabama, 1936. Courtesy of the Dorothea Lange Collection, The Oakland Museum. Gift of Paul S. Taylor.*
Lange often photographed only the hands or feet of her subjects. This image shows how important the hoe cutter's hands are to his work.

usually something that showed how life was changing for people under enormous financial pressures. Both she and Taylor believed that their best work came from spontaneous experiences. Stryker agreed.

From the federal office, the couple headed toward New Jersey to photograph and write about a government project whose aim was to resettle the families of garment workers who had lost their jobs in New York City. Next they drove through North Carolina, where Lange photographed poor laborers hoeing crops, then on through Tennessee, Florida, and Georgia, where peach pickers earned seventy-five cents a day.

Along the way, they sometimes saw other photographers who worked for Stryker. Lange always enjoyed meeting with them to discuss their photographic techniques. Outside of Birmingham, Alabama, an African-American tenant family of seven explained they earned only $150 a year for the labor of both adults and their five children.

Hoe Culture and *Ex-Slave with Long Memory* show the strength and determination of the people in the Alabama fields. Lange captured the texture of their weathered skin and tattered clothing by carefully focusing her camera lens. The ex-slave appears unposed, perhaps telling a painful tale of yesteryear. In *Hoe Culture,* however, Lange emphasizes the hard work that her subject does through a close-up shot of only his body and arms. In each image, the hands — the human connection to the tool of the land — are important to the meaning.

As Lange and Taylor moved through the South, the hot summer sun parched the soil. Newspapers and radio stations reported that the drought had caused crop losses of more than one hundred million dollars. *Six Tenant Farmers Without Farms* reflects

Dorothea Lange. **Ex-Slave with Long Memory.** *Alabama, 1937. Courtesy of the Dorothea Lange Collection, The Oakland Museum. Gift of Paul S. Taylor.*
This former slave gazes into the distant past, perhaps recalling painful memories.

hardships. In the Midwest, the wind blew topsoil off the fields. Huge dark clouds of dirt thickened the air until people couldn't see their own hands. Even porch lights were completely blackened. Much of the Midwest had become known as the Dust Bowl.

Dorothea Lange. **Six Tenant Farmers Without Farms.** *Hardaman County, Texas, 1938. Courtesy of the Dorothea Lange Collection, The Oakland Museum. Gift of Paul S. Taylor.*

Dorothea Lange. **Family on the Road.** *Oklahoma, 1938. Courtesy of the Dorothea Lange Collection, The Oakland Museum. Gift of Paul S. Taylor.*
Many families in the Dust Bowl lost their farms because they could not grow crops to pay for the land.

With no topsoil in parts of Texas and Oklahoma, thousands of farm families were left with no way to make a living. So they headed for California, where they had heard about the migrant workers' camps. Some families traveled by car, while others went by foot. *Family on the Road* shows a father and mother with their two children, likely trying to catch a ride to California.

As she did for *Family on the Road*, Lange knelt down to photograph *Woman of the High Plains*. By looking up at her subjects, the photographer created images that lend a sense of power to their being. In viewing these two images, we realize the inner strength of the poverty-stricken subjects, even though they appear destitute.

During Lange's years of photographing for the FSA, she was laid off more than once due to federal

Dorothea Lange. **Woman of the High Plains.** *Texas Panhandle, 1938. Courtesy of the Dorothea Lange Collection, The Oakland Museum. Gift of Paul S. Taylor.*
Lange's photographs, such as this one, show the inner strength of rural Americans who were faced with financial hardships.

funding cuts. But she always made good use of her time. In 1938, she and Taylor worked on a book of her photographs and his writings, *An American Exodus*, which described the plight of the migrant workers. By 1940, when the book reached the stores, however, the country's attention had shifted to preparation for World War II.

In that same year, the family moved from San Francisco to Berkeley. Lange's years of service for Stryker's FSA were over. Her massive collection of Depression-era photographs had gained national recognition. Her experience on Stryker's staff was the greatest education she could have received. In 1940, *Migrant Mother* was exhibited at the Museum of Modern Art in New York. Indeed, Lange had joined the ranks of master photographers.

Dorothea Lange. **One Nation Indivisible.** *San Francisco, 1942. Courtesy of the Dorothea Lange Collection, The Oakland Museum. Gift of Paul S. Taylor.*
The anxious facial expression of the Japanese-American schoolgirl (*front left*) saluting the American flag symbolizes the injustices that soon would come about.

On December 7, 1941, the United States was brought into the Second World War by the Japanese attack on Pearl Harbor. In response, President Roosevelt ordered that 110,000 Japanese-American women, men, and children be forced from their homes and moved into detention camps. Roosevelt feared they might leak secrets to relatives in Japan.

A new department of the federal government, the War Relocation Authority (WRA), hired Lange to document in photographs the migration of the Japanese-Americans to the detention camps. Indeed, it now seems odd that our government chose to record its own mistakes. But it is important to understand that our country's fear of Japan in 1942 caused government officials to believe that their decisions would protect our country. Unfortunately instead, they were demonstrating racial prejudice.

Dorothea Lange. **Two Women.** *Nepal, 1958. Courtesy of the Dorothea Lange Collection, The Oakland Museum. Gift of Paul S. Taylor.*
By filling the photograph's frame with her subjects, Lange created a feeling of intimacy, or closeness, between the subjects and the viewer.

From April to July 1942, Lange traveled with the thousands of evacuees on buses and trains to assembly centers and finally on to the detention camps. She took 760 photographs of this historic event. *One Nation Indivisible* was taken a few weeks before the evacuation began.

During the next fifteen years, Lange found herself in a variety of situations. She photographed for the government, recuperated from a lengthy illness, prepared for a second exhibit at the Museum of Modern Art in New York, and traveled with her son Daniel, who had grown up to become a writer.

From 1958 to 1962, Lange traveled with Taylor, whose assignments took them to Asia, Venezuela, Ecuador, and Egypt. Her fascination with people in their natural surroundings is reflected through the portraits she captured on film during these trips. In Korea, she took a portrait entitled *Children*, of four young boys peering through a window. *Two Women* is a portrait Lange took in Nepal, filling the entire frame of the picture with her subjects.

Dorothea Lange. **Children.** *Korea, 1958. Courtesy of the Dorothea Lange Collection, The Oakland Museum. Gift of Paul S. Taylor.*

29

Dorothea Lange. **Gunlock.**
*Utah, 1953. Courtesy of the
Dorothea Lange Collection,
The Oakland Museum. Gift of
Paul S. Taylor.*
Who would ever have
thought to pose a boy
halfway atop his horse?
Lange's talent helped her
envision this photograph as
she traveled through
Gunlock, Utah.

Dorothea Lange. **Andrew.**
*Berkeley, 1959. Courtesy of
the Dorothea Lange Collection,
The Oakland Museum. Gift of
Paul S. Taylor.*
Young Andrew's hands frame
his face. Light reflects from
them to highlight his smile.
Lange's style often
emphasized the hands or feet,
showing them to be as
expressive as the face.

During her later years, Lange stayed closer to home because her health began to fail. She presented photography seminars in San Francisco, published many of her photographs, and organized them for solo and group exhibitions at museums.

Gunlock and *Andrew*, two of her most prized photographs, appeared in the museum exhibits and continue to be published today.

Her fondest times in her later years were spent with her children and grandchildren at the family's cabin at Steep Ravine, on the Pacific coast. Finally, she was able to enjoy the pleasures of family life, as well as the joys of freedom from a busy schedule. At the cabin, she took many pictures of the children who loved to vacation there. *Leslie Dixon Reading at Steep Ravine* shows one of Lange's granddaughters enraptured by a book on a cool summer afternoon.

Toward the end of her life, Lange received many honors. She had solo exhibitions in Boston and Europe. Thirty years after the Great Depression, Americans were becoming curious about that era,

Dorothea Lange. **Leslie Dixon Reading at Steep Ravine.** *c. 1957. Courtesy of the Dorothea Lange Collection, The Oakland Museum. Gift of Paul S. Taylor.*
At the cabin, Lange and her grandchildren loved to experience nature, to be together, and to be alone. Her photographs of this special place are some of her best work — unposed subjects in spontaneous activity.

and group exhibitions across the United States included her work.

The last year of her life was unusually productive. She organized her photographs for a solo exhibit at the Museum of Modern Art in New York, which would open in January 1966. She completed her collection of pictures for the book *The American Country Woman*. She even worked on two films for the National Educational Television and Radio Center.

In August 1965, Lange was diagnosed with cancer. She reflected on her life. She was grateful for most everything that had happened to her. She found strength through it all — even from her bout with polio. She stated that polio was perhaps the most important thing that happened to her, that it formed her, instructed her, helped her, and humiliated her. She was aware of its force and power.

During her lifetime, she was considered an artist by many who knew her work. Lange knew that she had always had an artist's drive and the vision of possibility. She felt that she had worked from the secret places of her heart. Only during her later years, however, did she acknowledge that

Dorothea Lange. **Paul's Sixty-Second Birthday.** *1957. Courtesy of the Dorothea Lange Collection, The Oakland Museum. Gift of Paul S. Taylor.*
Taylor was forever devoted to Lange. Today her photographs are housed in the Library of Congress, the National Archives — and at the Oakland Museum, to whom Taylor donated more than twenty thousand negatives, prints, and pieces of memorabilia.

Rondal Partridge. **On the Beach at Steep Ravine.** *1940s. Copyright © Rondal Partridge, 1993.*

photography was indeed an art and she herself an artist.

Dorothea Lange died on October 11, 1965, at the age of seventy. The field of photography lost a masterful artist, yet it had gained the lasting contribution of a pioneer. She is remembered as one of the original documentary photographers, who used her camera as an instrument for social change.